LITHOGRAPHIC SKETCHES OF THE PUBLIC CHARACTERS OF CALCUTTA

LITHOGRAPHIC SKETCHES OF THE PUBLIC CHARACTERS OF CALCUTTA

C. GRANT

GYAN

Published by

GYAN

Gyan Publishing House
5, Ansari Road
Daryaganj, New Delhi-110002
Phone: 011-47034999, 9811692060
E-mail: books@gyanbooks.com

Distribution Network
gyanbooks.com
India, USA, Canada, UK, Australia

ISBN: 978-93-7133-506-5 (PB)

First Published, 1859

2nd Impression 2025

Printed at: Gyan Press, Delhi.

LITHOGRAPHIC SKETCHES OF THE PUBLIC CHARACTERS OF CALCUTTA
Author: C. GRANT

LITHOGRAPHIC SKETCHES OF THE PUBLIC CHARACTERS OF CALCUTTA.

BY

C. GRANT.

PUBLISHED IN THE "INDIA REVIEW," INDIA MEDICAL-" "CALCUTTA MONTHLY," AND "BENGAL SPORTING" JOURNALS, THE "CALCUTTA CHRISTIAN OBSERVER," AND "INDIA SPORTING REVIEW."

1833 TO 185

CALCUTTA:

W. THACKER AND CO. ST. ANDREW'S LIBRARY.

M

PORTRAIT SKETCHES

OF THE

PUBLIC CHARACTERS OF CALCUTTA.

PUBLISHED IN THE "INDIA REVIEW," "INDIA MEDICAL," "CALCUTTA MONTHLY," AND "BENGAL SPORTING" JOURNALS, THE "CALCUTTA CHRISTIAN OBSERVER," AND "INDIA SPORTING REVIEW."

From 1838 to 1850.

BY

COLESWORTHEY GRANT.

			Published in the	Date of Publcn.
1	DR. W. TWINING ..	Presidency Surgeon; Surgeon, General Hospital, Calcutta, 1833. Author of "The Clinical Diseases of India"	Ind. Med. Journ.	1838
2	DR. C. PEARS	Calcutta. A retired Medical Officer of the H. E. I. Co.'s Service. An enthusiastic Bibliophilist		
3	DR. W. O'SHAUGHNESSY ...	Professor of Chemistry, Med. Coll. Calcutta; Introducer of the Telegraph into India; now Sir W. O'Shaughnessy Brooke. Author of the Bengal Dispensatory," "Pharmacopœia," etc.	" "	
4	DR. FRED. CORBYN ...	Garrison Surgeon, Fort William, Calcutta; Editor of "India Med. Jour." & "India Review;" and Author of a Treatise on the Diseases of Children in India ...		1837
[illegible]	DR. C. C. EGERTON ..	Professor of Surgery and Clinical Surgery, Calcutta ...	" "	1838
	DR. N. WALLICH, F. R. S. ...	Professor of Botany, Med. College, Calcutta; Superintendent, Botanic Gardens	" "	
[illegible]	DR. H. H. GOODEVE ...	Professor of Anatomy and Medicine, Med. College, Calcutta. Author of "Hints on the Management of Children in India"	" "	
8	DAVID HARE, ESQ. ...	Watch and Clock Maker, of Calcutta, better known as the friend of Native Education, and latterly as a Commissioner of the Petty Debt Court in Calcutta. His biography by Baboo Peary Churn Mitter was lately published in Calcutta, and his Statue by Baily, R. A. is erected in the grounds of the Presidency College. The "Hare School" is so called after him ...	India Review.	1838
9	DR. W. JACOB, L. R. C.S.,D....	Bengal Medical Estabt. Author of "A short account of the District of Jessore," 1837. Of great reputation in Dum-Dum. Retired		
10	REV. THOMAS BOAZ, LL. D. ...	Editor of the "Cal. Christian Observer," and Founder of 'The Sailors' Home.' Indep. Minister, Union Chapel	Lect. on Popery.	
11	DR. J. T. PEARSON ...	Bengal Medl. Establishment	Medical Journal.	
12	M. M. MANUK, ESQ. .	Armenian Merchant	India Review.	1837
13	SIR BENJ. H. MALKIN ...	Judge, Supreme Court of Judicature, Bengal. Author of an excellent Treatise on Astronomy, published by the "Society for the Diffusion of Useful Knowledge"		1838
14	DR. WALTER RALEIGH ...	Surgeon, Cal. Gen. Hospital; Assist. Superintendent, Eye Infirmary. 1838	Medical Journal.	1838
15	SIR ED. RYAN, M. A. ...	Chief Justice, Supreme Court, Bengal, from 1833 to 1842. President, Asiatic Society: Mem. of H. M. Privy Council	India Review.	1838
16	J. H. STOCQUELER, ESQ. ...	Projector and Editor of the Calcutta "Englishman." From 18 to 18		
17	JOHN PEARSON, ESQ., M.A. ...	Advocate-General, Supreme Court, Bengal. 1838 ...		
18	CAPT. W. H. COCKERELL ...	Senior Partner, Messrs. Cockerell & Co., Merchants ...	Ben. Sport. Mag.	
19	C. E. TREVELYAN, C.S., SUBSEQUENTLY SIR CHAS. TREVELYAN	One time Governor of Madras, and afterwards (1863) Financial Member of Council to Supreme Government, Bengal	India Review.	
20	DR. (THE LATE SIR) RANALD MARTIN	Presidency Surgeon, and Surgeon, Native Hospital, Calcutta. Author of the "Diseases of Tropical Climates." Latterly President or Chairman of the Home Medical Board	Medical Journal.	

			Published in the	Date of Publicn.
21	A. H. Larpent, Esq. ...	Merchant of Calcutta (now Sir A. H. Larpent, Bart.) ...	Beng. Sport. Mag.	
22	Sir Charles (afterwards Lord) Metcalfe, G.C.B. ...	Formerly of Jamaica. Pro tem. (from 20th March 1835 to 4th March 1836) Governor-General of India. The Liberator of the Indian Press	India Review.	
23	Capt. D. L. Richardson ...	Author of Literary Leaves in Prose and Verse, "Ocean Sketches," and other Poems. Principal of the Hindu College	C. Monthly Jrnl.	1838
24	Dr. Simon Nicolson ...	Surgeon, Presidency Surgeon, General Hospital. For 50 years a Practitioner in Calcutta	Medical Journal.	1838
25	Sir J. P. Grant, M.A. ...	Judge, Supreme Court, Calcutta ...	India Review.	1838
26	James Sutherland, Esq. ...	Editor, "Bengal Hurkaru." Secretary to the Marine Board, Bengal. With Dr. John Grant, D. L. Richardson, H. M. Parker, and J. W. Kaye one of the Literary coterie of their day	C. Monthly Jrnl.	1838
27	Dr. John Grant ...	Surgeon, Beng. Med. Service. Author of many Literary Productions. Apothecary-General, H. E. I. Co.'s Service. From 1840 to 1848, District. Grand Master of Freemasons, Bengal	Medical Journal.	1838
28	W. Hickey, Esq. ...	Merchant of Calcutta	Beng. Sport. Mag.	1838
29	Longueville Clarke, Esq., M.A., F.R.S.	Barrister-at-Law, Supreme Court, Bengal. Died at Rangoon, 1863	India Review.	1838
30	J. W. Kaye, Esq. (The late Sir J. W. Kaye) ...	Editor, "Literary Gazette." Author of the "Sepoy War," &c.	C. Monthly Jrnl.	1838
31	J. F. Leith, Esq. ...	Barrister-at-Law, Supreme Court, Bengal. Secretary, India Office, Political Department	India Review.	1838
32	C. Newcomen, Esq. ...	Merchant, Firm of Messrs. Cockerell & Co., Calcutta ...	Beng. Sport. Mag.	1838
33	Dr. Henry H. Spry, F.G.S., M.R.A.S.	Author of "Modern India"	India Review.	1838
34	Capt. R. A. Macnaughten ..	Editor of the 'Englishman,' author of "An Essay on Military Laws," &c., and a History of the campaigns of the army under Gen. Adams	" "	1838
35	Mr. Tom Pitts ...	Firm of Messrs. Cook & Co.	Beng. Sport. Mag.	
36	Major J. R. Colnett, 11th B.N.I.	Fort Adjutant, Fort William. The real Hero of the oft-told tale of a Bengal Officer carried off by a Tiger ...	India Review.	1838
37	Rev. Henry Fisher ...	Senior Chaplain, Bengal Ecclesiastical Establishment ...	" "	1838
38	Rev. J. Penney ...	Baptist Mission. Founder, or chief Promoter, and Head Master of the Benevolent Institution ...		1838
39	H. T. Prinsep, Esq., C.S. ...	Author of a Narrative of Political and Military Transactions of British India, &c.; Member of the Supreme Council, Calcutta; Afterwards Director of the H. E. I. Company. Subsequently Member of the Council of the Sec. of State for India	" "	1838
40	Capt. Maling	Bengal Army	Beng. Sport. Mag.	
41	Rajah Pertab Chund ...	The "Claimant" of the Burdwan Raj	India Review.	1838
42	John Clarke Marshman, Esq., C.S.I.	Editor of the "Friend of India." Author of a "History of India," &c.	" "	1838
43	Jas. Prinsep, Esq., F.R.S ...	Secretary, Asiatic Society, &c. Assay Master, first at Benares, afterwards Calcutta Mint. Secretary to the Asiatic Society, Calcutta. Well-known as a Philologist, Numismatist, and Antiquarian. Author of "Benares Illustrated," &c.	" "	1838
44	T. Holroyd, Esq. ...	Merchant	Beng. Sport. Mag.	
45	Capt. W. Long ...	Formerly Commandant in the Mahratta Army, &c. ...	India Review	1838
46	Major Carter ...	Bengal Army	Beng. Sport. Mag.	
47	C. B. Greenlaw, Esq. ...	Coroner of Calcutta; one time Editor of the "Bengal Harkaru"	India Review.	1838
48	G. W. Bacon, Esq. ...	B. C. S.	Beng. Sport. Mag.	-
49	Dr. J. Hutchison, Bengal Medical Service ...	Author of "The Sunyassee," &c., and other Poems ...	In. Med. Journal.	1839
50	C. Butcher, Esq. ...	... ...	Beng. Sport. Mag.	
51	Capt. T. J. Taylor, R.E. ...	Bengal Army	India Review.	
52	Rt. Rev. Daniel Wilson, D.D.	Lord Bishop of Calcutta, from 1832 till 1857. Author of several works on Christian Divinity ...	" "	
53	J. White, Esq. ...	Indigo Planter, Kishnaghur District	Beng. Sport. Mag.	
54	Hon. C. H. Cameron ...	India Law Commission, and Member of the Supreme Council	India Review.	1839
55	Theodore Dickens, Esq. ...	Barrister-at-Law, Calcutta	" "	1839

			Published in the	Dated of Publican.
56	C. W. Smith, Esq., B.C.S.	Captain of the Bengal Archers	India Review.	1839
57	Sir Thomas E. M. Turton, Bart.	Barrister-at-Law, Calcutta, and Administrator-General	" "	1839
58	H. M. Parker, Esq., B.C.S.	Author of "Bole Ponjis," and of Miscellaneous Poems	" "	1839
59	Percy Eld, Esq.	Bengal Army	Beng. Sport. Mag.	1839
60	R. H. Rattray, Esq., B.C.S.	Author of "The Exile" and other Poems. Judge of the Sudder Dewany Court	India Review.	1839
61	F. W. Gryles, Esq.	...	Beng. Sport. Mag.	
62	Rev. W. H. Carey	Baptist Missionary, Cutwa, Burdwan	India Review.	1840
63	D. W. Fraser, Esq.	Known as "Coolie Fraser"	Beng. Sport. Mag.	
64	H. Piddington, Esq	Coroner of Calcutta. Author of a work on the Law of Storms	India Review.	1840
65	W. H. L. Frith, Esq.	Solicitor of Calcutta	Beng. Sport. Mag.	1840
66	Rev. W. O. Ruspini	Chaplain, Bengal Ecclesiastical Establishment	India Review.	
67	Capt. R. Thornton	Commander of the "Thomas Granville"	Beng. Sport. Mag.	1840
68	Major Eldred Pottinger, C.B.	"The Hero of Charekar," 1840, and Defender of Herat	India Review.	
69	Capt. A. H. E. Boileau	Bengal Engineers. Author of a Tour through Rajwara in 1835. Afterwards General Boileau. District Grand Master of Bengal (Freemasons) 1862	" "	
70	Richard Lawry, Esq.	...	Beng. Sport. Mag.	
71	E. Kent Hume, Esq.	Brother to James Hume, Esq....	" "	
72	Dr. Strong	Bengal Medical Service. One of the earliest advocates of Sanitary Reform in Calcutta. At one time in charge of the Lunatic Asylum	India Review.	
73	Col. G. Warren	Commandant, Fort William, Calcutta	" "	1840
74	Dr. James Burnes, K.G.H., F.R.S.	Author of "A visit to the Court of Sinde." Brother to Sir Alexander Burnes	" "	
75	Capt. J. T. Boileau	Bengal Engineers. Now General Boileau. For some years in charge of the Magnetical Observatory at Simla	" "	
76	Col. D. McLeod	Bengal Engineers. Father of Sir Donald McLeod	" "	1841
77	Dr. J. McClelland	Professor, Medical College, and Editor of the "Calcutta Journal of Natural History," &c.	Ind. Med. Journ.	
78	W. F. Fergusson, Esq.	Firm of Messrs. Fergusson Brothers & Co., Merchants of Calcutta	Beng. Sport. Mag.	
79	Dr. F. H. Brett	Surgeon, Governor-General's Bodyguard, and Surgeon, Eye Infirmary	Ind. Med. Journ.	
80	Sir Gordon Bremer, K.B., K.C.H.	Commodore, H. M. Navy	India Review.	1841
81	Mr. R. Ross.	Firm of Messrs. Cook & Co.	Sport. Review.	
82	Theodore Cantor, Esq.	Bengal Medical Service. A Dane. An eminent Naturalist. Founder of the "Cantor Lectures" delivered yearly at the Society of Arts, London	India Review.	1841
83	The Rev. Dr. Alexander Duff	Missionary. The great leader in Educational reform. Founder of the Free Church Institution	" "	1841
84	Capt. M. Kittoe	Bengal Engineers. Architect of the Benares College. Author of various articles on Antiquarian Researches in Upper India	" "	1841
85	C. K. Robinson, Esq.	Magistrate of Calcutta. Architect of the Ochterlony Monument and Metcalfe Hall	" "	1841
86	Major FitzGerald	Bengal Engineers ...	" "	1841
87	Rev. A. F. Lacroix	Missionary to the Hindoos. Lon. Missionary Society...	Lect. on Popery.	1841
88	Rev. H. S. Fisher	Chaplain of Fort William, Calcutta	India Review.	1841
89	Sir Richmond Shakespear	Political Agent, Court of Holkar. The Rescuer of the Cabul captives in 1842	" "	1842
90	Capt. A. Charlton	Bengal Army. Received Medal for discovery of the Assam Tea Plant	" "	1842
91	Rt. Hon. George Earl of Auckland, G.C.	Governor-General of India, from 1836 to 1838	" "	1842
92	Major E. D'Arcy Todd	Bengal Artillery. A Traveller in Central Asia when travellers there were rare. Killed at the Battle of Moodkee in 1845...	" "	1842
93	Major W. Hough, D.J.A.G.	Bengal Army. Author of a Narrative of the Operations of the Army of the Indus. 1839-40	" "	
94	Brigadier Anquetil	42nd N. I. Killed in the disastrous Retreat from Cabul. 1842	" "	
95	Rev. C. Arratoon	An Armenian Baptist Missionary		
96	Nuwab of Moorshedabad when young	Now in England	Private.	1842

			Published in the	Date of Publican.
97	Hon. A. Amos ...	India Law Commission	India Review.	1842
98	Lt.-Col. W. R. Pogson ...	Bengal Army. Author of "Scriptural and Historical Researches"	„ „	1846
99	H. Torrens, Esq., B.C.S. ...	Political Agent or Resident of Moorshedabad ...	„ „	1842
100	Rev. K. M. Bannerjea. ...	Bengal Ecclesiastical Establishment ...	„ „	1842
101	Lt.-Col. R. Powney. ...	Bengal Artillery, Commandant, Fort William, Calcutta	„ „	1842
102	Rev. Dr. W. Yates. ...	Baptist Missionary. Author of an Introduction to Hindustani and Bengali	Lect. on Popery.	1843
103	J. Stocqueler, Esq., as Iago.			
104	Geo. Thomson, Esq. ...	M. P. for the Tower Hamlets	India Review.	1843
105	Lt.-Gen. Sir Hugh Gough	Afterwards Lord Gqugh. Commander-in-Chief in India, 1843-49	„ „	1843
106	Ven. Archdeacon Dealtry, LL.D.	Formerly Archdeacon of Calcutta. Afterwards Bishop of Madras	„ „	1843
107	Capt. Geo. St. T. Lawrence	Bengal Cavalry. One of the Cabul Captives. Brother to Lord Lawrence and Sir H. Lawrence ...	„ „	1845
108	Rev. Wm. Morton ...	Formerly a Minister of the Church of England, and subsequently of the London Missionary Society ...	Lect. on Popery.	1845
109	General Avitabille ..	An Italian. Governor of Peshawur, under Reign of Runjeet Sing		
110	Rev. G. Mundy ...	Missionary, London Missionary Society ...	India Review.	1844
111	Colonel Wm. Burlton ...	District Grand Master (Freemasons), Bengal, 1851 to 1854	Private.	1845
112	Rev. W. H. Denham ...	Baptist Missionary, and Principal, Serampore College ...	Lect. on Popery.	1845
113	Rev. Thos. Smith ...	Minister of Free Kirk of Scotland. For some time Editor of the "Calcutta Review"	„ „	1845
114	Rev. J. Macdonald ...	Minister of Free Kirk of Scotland	„ „	1845
115	Rev. Dr. Charles ...	Senior Chaplain, St. Andrew's Church, Calcutta ...		
116	Rev. D. Ewart ...	Minister, Free Kirk of Scotland	Lect. on Popery.	
117	Lt.-Gen. Sir Charles Jas. Napier, G.C.B. ...	The Conqueror of Sindh, 1849-50. Commander-in-Chief in India	Mawson's Records.	
118	Mr. Geo. Barker ...	Jockey	Sport. Review.	1845
119	... ...	... ...		
120	J. H. Patton, Esq., B.C.S. ...	Judge of the Sudder Dewany Court	„ „	1846
121	J. Beckwith, Esq. ..	Merchant, Firm of Messrs. Fergusson Brothers & Co....	Ind. Sport. Revw.	1846
122	J. Bracken, Esq., B.C.S. ..	Collector of Customs, Calcutta	„ „	1846
123	W. P. Grant, Esq., B.C.S. ...	... ...	„ „	1846
124	Capt. Jas. Abbott (now General)	Bengal Artillery. Author of "The Thakoorine" (a Poem) and "Narrative of a Journey to Khiva" ...	India Review.	
125	Dr. J. Sawers ...	Bengal Medical Service	Ind. Sport. Revw.	1847
126	Mr. Wm. Hall ...	Jockey	„ „	1847
127	J. Stainforth, Esq., B.C.S...	Member of the Board of Revenue, Calcutta ...	„ „	1847
128	G. A. Bushby, Esq., B.C.S. ...	Secretary to the Govt. of India, and subsequently Resident at Hydrabad	„ „ „ „	1848 1848
129	W. Bracken, Esq. ...	... ...	Ben. Sport. Mag.	1849
130	W. H. L. Frith, Esq. ...	Solicitor, Calcutta	Ind. Sport. Revw.	1849
131	Shaik Ibrahim Bin Ullee	An Arab Horse-dealer	„ „	1849
132	G. Plowden, Esq., B.C.S. ...	Sec. to the Board of Revenue. Commissioner of Burdwan	„ „	1849
133	Ubdool Ruhman ...	An Arab Horse-dealer	„ „	1849
134	Wm. Pybus, Esq. ...	Artist	Ind. Sport. Revw.	1849
135	Sir John Cheape, C.B. ...	Commanding forces in the 2nd Burmese War ...	„ „	1850
136	James Grant, Esq., B.C.S. ...	Civil and Session Judge of Dinagepore	„ „	1850
137	J. Johnstone, Esq. ...	Merchant, Calcutta	„ „	1850
138	James Hume, Esq. ...	"Abel East." Editor of the "India Sporting Review;" Proprietor and Editor of "Eastern Star," &c.; and Magistrate of Calcutta	„ „	1850
139	Wm. Grey, Esq., B.C.S. ...	Afterwards Sir Wm. Grey, Lieut.-Governor of Bengal...	„ „	1850
140	A. Moffat Mills, Esq., B.C.S.	Chief Magistrate of Calcutta and Judge of the Sudder Dewany Court	„ „	1851
141	Major Rowland, Hill ...	Irregular Cavalry	„ „	1851
142	Major-Genl. Sir Walter Raleigh Gilbert, G.C.B....	Commander of Advanced Division in the 2nd Punjab War	„ „	1851
143	Thomas Brown, Esq. ...	Head Partner, Firm of Messrs. Hunter & Co. ...	„ „	1852
144	Major C. B. Chalmers ...	Bengal Cavalry	„ „	1852
145	Charles Prinsep, Esq. ...	Barrister-at-Law, Calcutta. Advocate-General ...	„ „	1852
146	Mr. Nicholas O'Brien ...	A respected old Police Officer, familiarly known as "Agé Burou" ("Move on")	„ „	1853

			Published in the	Date of Publicn.
147	Dr. Norman Chevers ...	Beng. Med. Service. Principal Medical College. Author of a work in high repute on "Indian Medical Jurisprudence," "Humanity in War," &c.		
148	The Rev. Dr. Charles ...	Minister of St. Andrew's Church, Calcutta ...		
149	The Rev. Dr. Meiklejohn	Do. do. do.		
150	Genl. Sir G. Pollock, G.C.B.	Royal Artillery, Commander of the "Avenging Army in Cabul; subsequently Resident of Lucknow. Brother to Sir Fred. Pollock, Chief Baron of the Exchequer..		
151	Sirdar Dost Mohummud Khan	The Umeer or Ruler of Afghanistan in 1840 ...	Oriental Heads.	1841
152	Gholam Hyder Khan ...	Fourth son of Dost Mohummud Khan. The Defender of Ghuzni	" "	1841 1841
153	Mohummud Ukrum Khan ...	Third son of Dost Mohummud Khan	" "	
154	Sree Jung Buhadur ...	Prime Minister and Commander-in-Chief of Nepal ..	Not Published.	
155	. . . .	Brother to Jung Bahadur	" "	
156	. . . .	Second brother to do.	" "	
157	Dr. Frederick J. Mouat ...	Beng. Med. Service. Secretary to the Board of Education; Inspector-General of Jails; Director of Public Instruction. Author of A Trip to Rèunion, &c. ...	" "	
158	H. H. Meer Mohummud Nusser Khan, Umeer of Sindh	The Principal Umeer, who Commanded at the Battle of Meanee	" "	
159	H. H. Meer Mohummud Khan, 2nd Umeer of Do.	... ...	" "	
160	H. H. Meer Sobhdar Khan, 3rd Umeer of Do.	... ...	" "	
161	Baboo Russamoy Dutt ...	Judge of the Small Cause Court, Calcutta ...	Private.	
162	Maharajah Kalee Krishna	... ...	Oriental Heads.	
163	Rustomjee Cowasjee, Esq.	Parsee Merchant of Calcutta	" "	
164	O'Hanlon	Commissioner of the Cal. Petty (Debt) Court. ...	Private.	
165	Major Showers ...	Tutor to the Young Nawab Nazim of Moorshedabad. Afterwards commanding 1st Bengal Fusilliers at the Siege of Delhi, and in Command of the Presidency Division	" "	
166	Dr. Forsyth	Surgeon, Calcutta Presidency	" "	
167	Jas. Forlong, Esq. ...	Manager of the Bengal Indigo Company, Mulnath, Kishnaghur	" "	1844

DWFraser

The Right Revd Daniel Wilson. D.D. Lord Bishop of Calcutta.

D Calcutta

The Revd
Wm Morton

Henry H. Spry

MD. FGS. MRAS.

Author of 'Modern India'.

"Touch me not so near:" — Act 1st Scene 3d

James Burnes

K.C.H. F.R.S.

Captn Geo St Lawrence

Yrs faithfully
H W Parker

Lieut. Colonel

Yrs faithfully
H W Parker

C.G.
Bengal Sporting Magazine
Calcutta Nov.
1835

J. Sawers

Thos. E. M. Turton

Supreme Court. Bengal.

G. Warren.

C.G.
from Sport. Review
Calcutta July 1851.
Irreg. Cavalry
Major,

The Revd W Yates D.D.

C.G.
Calcutta April 1841.

Theodore Dickens

Supreme Court, Bengal.

C.G.
Calcutta
Sporting Review
March

C.G.
India Review, Calcutta

The Honble Andw. Amos.

C.G.
W Hale

CG
INDIA REVIEW

THE HON^BLE^ SIR J. P. GRANT.
Supreme Court of Judicature. Bengal.

Formerly on the Bench of Bombay.

———— "a man so bold,
That dares do Justice" ————

THE RIGHT HONORABLE GEORGE EARL OF

Auckland

G.C.B. &c.

Sir
Lieut. General
Bart: G.C.B. K.C.S.
C.G.
Calcutta
May 43.

The Rev.d W. Carey. Culwa.

Genl Avitabile
(Late Governor of Peshawur)
C.G.
Calcutta

WALTER RALEIGH ESQR.

First Assistant Surgeon Calcutta General Hospital,

Assistant Superintendent, Eye Infirmary &c &c.

C.S.
India Sportg. Review
Calcutta . Sep. 1850
James Hume

India Law Commission.

C.G.
Calcutta
Novr. 1842

C.S.
INDIA SPORT REVIEW
Calcutta
Dec. 1850.

R H Rattray B.C.S.

Author of "The Exile" and other Poems.

D. L. Richardson

Author of "Literary Leaves" – "Ocean Sketches" &c.

The Revd. Alexander Duff D.D.

C.G. Calcutta 1842
Major E. D'Arcy Todd

The Revd.

LONGUEVILLE L. CLARKE ESQRE M.A. F.R.S.

Supreme Court of Judicature, Bengal.

R Ross

The Revd. Thomas Boaz

SIR
K.B. KCH &c

Nicholas O'Brien

The Revd. A. F. Lacroix

Missionary to the Hindoos.

C.G.
Calcutta
August 1842.

C. G.
Calcutta, Mar. 1841.
ZENOBIA
Yours truly G J Dennes

Dr. Frederick Corbyn

The Revd. H. S. Fisher

Yours very faithfully
Adam Freer Smith.

Danl. Madras

C.G.
INDIA REVIEW
Geo. Thompson

Eldred Pottinger C.B.

C.G. Calcutta
May 1843
SOPHIA